SUPERIOR ANIMAL SENSES

HOW
ELEPHANTS
AND OTHER ANIMALS
HEAR THE EARTH

Caitie McAneney

PowerKiDS press.

New York

Published in 2016 by The Rosen Publishing Group, Inc.
29 East 21st Street, New York, NY 10010

First Edition

Editor: Katie Kawa
Book Design: Reann Nye

Photo Credits: Cover Gallo Images - Daryl Balfour/Riser/Getty Images; p. 5 Catfish Photography/Shutterstock.com; p. 7 Lenaa Livaya/Shutterstock.com; p. 9 Villiers Steyn/Shutterstock.com; pp. 11, 21 (elephant) john michael evan potter/ Shutterstock.com; p. 12 Nancy Tripp Photography/Shutterstock.com; p. 13 skynetphoto/Shutterstock.com; pp. 15, 21 (snake) Aleksei Verhovski/ Shutterstock.com; p. 17 (top) Ryan M. Bolton/Shutterstock.com; p. 17 (bottom) Thomas Marent/Minden Pictures/Getty Images; pp. 18, 21 (mole) Gary Meszaros/ Science Source/Getty Images; p. 19 Wayne Lynch/All Canada Photos/Getty Images; p. 21 (spider) kurt_G/Shutterstock.com; p. 22 Julian W/Shutterstock.com.

Library of Congress Cataloging-in-Publication Data

McAneney, Caitie.
How elephants and other animals hear the earth / by Caitie McAneney.
p. cm. — (Superior animal senses)
Includes index.
ISBN 978-1-4994-0991-8 (pbk.)
ISBN 978-1-4994-1030-3 (6 pack)
ISBN 978-1-4994-1065-5 (library binding)
1. Sound production by animals — Juvenile literature. 2. Hearing — Juvenile literature. 3. Perception in animals — Juvenile literature. I. McAneney, Caitlin. II. Title.
QL765.M34 2016
591.59'4—d23

Manufactured in the United States of America

CPSIA Compliance Information: Batch #WS15PK: For Further Information contact Rosen Publishing, New York, New York at 1-800-237-9932

CONTENTS

VIBRATING EARTH

Over time, animals **adapt** to their surroundings, which helps them survive. Some animals have supersenses that help them stay away from harm and **communicate** with others. A very special sense is the ability to "hear" the earth.

What does it mean to hear the earth? Some animals can feel small movements in the ground, which are called vibrations or seismic (SYZ-mihk) waves. These animals may have special body parts that help them pick up on these vibrations. Elephants have this supersense. Through the ground, they can sense the rumblings of an elephant call or the vibrations of an approaching animal.

THAT MAKES SENSE!

An elephant's call is so deep and low that the sound can sometimes travel farther through the ground than the air. This kind of deep elephant call is also known as a rumble.

Sensing vibrations in the ground is a major way elephants communicate. They also communicate by moving their bodies in certain ways, much like people using sign language.

COMMUNICATION IS IMPORTANT

There are two species, or kinds, of elephants—the African elephant and the Asian elephant. African elephants are the largest land animals in the world. They live throughout Africa. Asian elephants are slightly smaller, with smaller and more rounded ears. This book will focus on African elephants.

African elephants eat a lot—up to 300 pounds (136 kg) of food a day! They need to travel far to find so much food and water. While male elephants often **roam** alone, females and young elephants roam in groups called herds. Elephants in a herd keep each other safe. Communication is very important in elephant herds.

THAT MAKES SENSE!

The size of an African elephant and its place in a herd help keep it safe from predators. However, elephants that are weak, lost, or alone are at risk of being attacked by animals such as lions and crocodiles.

People who study elephants notice they have very close **relationships** within their herd. Elephants in a herd can recognize one another, even after being separated. They also recognize calls from elephants they know.

ELEPHANT CALLS AND FOOT STOMPING

Elephants often call to one another. They can cry and roar. They can also make loud sounds like a trumpet. Their voices can rumble deeply. Each call means something different, and other elephants know what each call means. This helps them communicate and work as a team. When an elephant's call rumbles through the ground, other elephants can feel the vibrations from it.

Elephants also stomp, or stamp, their feet to communicate. They might stomp their feet to warn other elephants when there's danger. The foot stomps of these heavy creatures pass through the ground as vibrations other elephants can sense.

THAT MAKES SENSE!

Scientists believe elephants listen most carefully and **react** most strongly to warning calls from other elephants they know.

When elephants sense certain vibrations through the ground, they stand closer to their group. This gets them ready to run away from an attack together if necessary.

SENSING VIBRATIONS

How can elephants sense vibrations in the ground? Elephants have large bones in their ears that may help them sense vibrations and hear low sounds. They can hear sounds too low for humans to hear.

An elephant's greatest tools for **detecting** vibrations in the ground are their feet and trunk. They touch the ground with their feet and trunk, and they feel the vibrations through special sensors in those body parts. Elephants lean forward on their front legs when they feel vibrations in the ground. This may help them pick up on faraway movements. Elephants can detect warning vibrations coming from miles away!

THAT MAKES SENSE!

Scientists believe elephants are able to sense earthquakes before they happen because they can so easily detect seismic waves. An earthquake is a shaking of a part of the earth.

Scientists can tell that an elephant is detecting vibrations just by the way it stands. Elephants might turn to face the direction of the sound to hear it more clearly.

SPIDER SENSES

Elephants aren't the only animals that can sense vibrations. Some species of spider use vibrations to communicate with possible **mates**. They also use vibrations to tell when there's an insect nearby. What's their spider secret?

Spiders use their webs to create vibrations. Spider webs are spun out of strong silk made by a spider's body. A spider spins a web to trap **prey**. Scientists know that spiders pull the strings of their web. It makes a vibration the spider can use to tell if there's something in their web, such as a mate or meal.

THAT MAKES SENSE!

Spiders can't see very well. That makes their ability to sense vibrations in their web even more important. Without their special sense, they wouldn't know if a bug was trapped in their web.

Male jumping spiders find mates by drumming their feet against the ground and vibrating certain body parts. Female jumping spiders sense these vibrations and then mate with the males.

SLITHERING SNAKES

Snakes don't have ears on the sides of their head like people and elephants do. Instead, snakes have inner ears that sense vibrations in the ground. Scientists think vibrations in the ground hit a snake's jawbone, which is connected to its inner ears. The jawbone is the bone that forms the mouth of the snake.

Detecting vibrations is very important for a snake. It helps the snake know when there's a predator in the area. It also helps the snake hunt for animals that are moving nearby. Scientists believe snakes can detect sounds in the air if the sounds are loud enough to make strong vibrations.

THAT MAKES SENSE!

Humans have eardrums, which help pick up vibrations from sounds in the air before they reach the inner ears. Snakes have inner ears, but no eardrums.

Snakes also have special sense **organs** along their body that can sense vibrations.

FROG TALK

Some frogs can communicate through vibrations in the ground. Scientists have studied the calls of the Caribbean white-lipped frog. They found the male frogs "sing" to get a mate. They also sit half-buried in the mud while they sing. Why do they do this?

As the frog sits in the mud to sing, its **vocal sacs** get bigger. When the vocal sacs move in the mud, they make a vibration that can be sensed by other frogs up to 20 feet (6 m) away. Scientists think these vibrations tell other males not to get too close when they're all **competing** for a mate.

THAT MAKES SENSE!

Small animals, such as frogs, spiders, and insects, often sense vibrations in the ground. That's because they're close to the ground. Vibrations we can't feel might feel like an earthquake to them!

Frogs are small enough to easily detect vibrations in the ground.

Rodents That Drum

Some animals, such as the kangaroo rat, use drumming to communicate. Drumming is hitting the ground over and over to make vibrations. This is like elephant foot stomping. Kangaroo rats drum with their feet. By drumming, they can tell others when predators are near. Kangaroo rats use vibrations to warn their babies when they sense danger.

Some species of mole rats also use drumming, except they use their heads! These mole rats are blind. They thump their heads against their underground tunnel walls to communicate with others. They may also use this drumming for **echolocation** to tell what's around them.

THAT MAKES SENSE!

The star-nosed mole has a nose with 22 tentacles that pick up on vibrations in the ground around them. Tentacles are long, thin body parts.

Foot drumming in kangaroo rats can help them warn others that a predator is near. These little rats have more in common with a big elephant than you probably thought!

Good Vibrations

Animals that use vibrations to communicate can pick up on many movements around them. However, humans can sometimes be a danger to animals with these supersenses, especially elephants.

Many elephants live in parks or reserves, which are places where they can roam freely and safely. If an elephant reserve is too close to human activity, the sounds and vibrations made by humans might block their communication. Loud zoos, especially ones close to busy roads, may also be harmful places for elephants to live because there are too many vibrations around them. People can help by making sure elephants have plenty of room in parks and reserves. They can also make sure elephants in zoos have a quiet place to live.

AFRICAN ELEPHANT
feet
trunk
ears

STAR-NOSED MOLE
tentacles

BODY PARTS USED TO HEAR THE EARTH

SPIDER
legs

SNAKE
jawbone

A Supersense!

Elephants and other animals that hear the earth have a supersense! Some animals can sense vibrations that come from many miles away. That's why these animals often know about earthquakes before they happen.

Communicating through vibrations is an animal skill that's been used for millions of years. Many bugs and other small animals have this ability, making it a popular form of communication in the animal world. Next time you're outside in a quiet place, put your hands on the ground. See if you can pick up on any vibrations, such as the rumble of a car. If you sit quietly enough, can you hear the earth?

This elephant is using its supersense to "hear" the ground through its feet and trunk.

GLOSSARY

adapt: To change to fit new conditions.

communicate: To share knowledge or feelings.

compete: To try to get something that another also wants.

detect: To notice something.

echolocation: The ability to locate faraway objects by sending sound waves and sensing them as they bounce off of the object.

mate: One of two animals that come together to make babies; also, to come together to make babies.

organ: A part of the body that has its own job.

prey: An animal hunted by other animals for food.

react: To do something because of something else that happens.

relationship: A connection between two or more things.

roam: To travel over a wide area without direction.

vocal sac: In male frogs, a loose fold of skin near the mouth that can be filled with air to make sound.

INDEX

WEBSITES

Due to the changing nature of Internet links, PowerKids Press has
developed an online list of websites related to the subject of this
book. This site is updated regularly. Please use this link to access
the list: www.powerkidslinks.com/sas/ele